Brownie Badge Book

Girlguiding UK
girls in the lead

www.girlguiding.org.uk

Published by
Girlguiding UK
17–19 Buckingham Palace Road
London
SW1W 0PT
Phone 020 7834 6242
Fax 020 7828 8317
Email chq@girlguiding.org.uk
Website www.girlguiding.org.uk
Girlguiding UK is an operating name of The Guide Association.
Incorporated by Royal Charter. Registered charity number 306016.
ISBN 978 0 85260 184 6
Trading Service ordering code 6801
Brownie Renewal Project Manager Anne Moffat
Senior Project Editor Alice Forbes
Writer Elizabeth Duffey
Special Project Designer David Jones
Design Team Janie Barton, Catherine Summers
Badges illustrated by Andi Good
Printed and bound by Paul Green Printing
© The Guide Association 2003
This edition © The Guide Association 2008
These badges resulted from the work of the Brownie Development Group:
Sandra Moffitt (Brownie Adviser, 1999–2004),
Helen Channa (Brownie Programme Coordinator),
Julia Bennett, Jean Bowers, Gillian Chalmers, Anne Hodder, Emmeline Kirton,
Alison Medler, Kirsty Thorburn and Catherine Watson.
The 2008 edition resulted from a process of ongoing review overseen
by Sue Waller (Brownie Adviser).
Girlguiding UK would like to thank all the Brownies and their Leaders who took part in the
consultations and pilot schemes for the development of the Brownie Adventure.
Users are reminded that during the lifespan of this publication there may be changes to:
• Girlguiding UK's policy
• legal requirements
• practice by governing bodies, for example the British Canoe Union
• British Standards
which will affect the accuracy of the information contained within these pages.
Throughout this book the terms 'parent' and 'daughter' are used. They apply equally
to a guardian or other adult with parental responsibility, and their ward.

Visit the Brownie website at www.girlguiding.org.uk/brownies

Contents

What this book is about

One of the great things about being a Brownie is having lots of different badges to try. Brownie badges cover many hobbies and interests, so you should be able to find some that you would like to do. Don't worry if you don't want to do any, as you don't have to do badges to be a Brownie. You can do as many or as few as you want, but it's best to only do one at a time.

Choosing a badge

All the Brownie badges you can do are in this book. Look at the contents list to see all their names.

When you have chosen one, look up what you need to do then talk with one of your Brownie Leaders about it.

You may pick a badge about one of your hobbies or something you already do well. You can also do a badge to start a new hobby or to see if you enjoy a new interest.

Advanced badges

Some interests and hobbies have got an advanced badge, too. It tells you at the start of the badge information if you need to have the first badge before trying it.

With your Brownie friends

You can do badges by yourself or with other Brownie friends. Sometimes your whole Pack or Six will do a badge together. If you do a badge with other Brownies, you still need to complete every part of it yourself and, of course, do your very best!

Doing your best

One of the most important things about being a Brownie is always doing your best at everything you try. Any part of a Brownie badge can be changed so you can show how you do your best. You may be set another clause that is just as hard. Some badges have been specially highlighted with a reminder that this can be done, though for some badges this won't be possible. If you want, the badge can be tested using your first language, if this is not English. Remember this is your choice.

> Whatever you do should be a challenge and you will always need to do your best!

Your own efforts

What you do for your badge must be your own work. You may need a little help with some parts of the badge, or **Be safe** you may need an adult you know to be with you so you are safe. Some parts of badges must be done with adult help. You'll see this sign to remind you.

How to get your badge

Your Leader will check that you have done all parts of your badge. She may ask an expert to make sure you have done everything properly. For some badges you might have to see more than one expert, or do different parts of the badge at different times. This is only to make sure what you do is checked fairly for you.

Take your pick

For some badges there is a choice of what you do. To make it clear it says whether you need to do all the options, or if you can choose which parts to do. Your Leader will help you make sure you have completed all you need to do for the badge you are trying.

Who is it that checks?

The person who checks you've done everything properly will usually be someone you know. It may be a teacher, the instructor at the club where you do your hobby, or one of your Brownie Leaders. When the tester is happy you have done your best at everything, you can ask him or her to sign to show you have completed the badge. Don't worry if they don't, as you will still get the badge once your Leader has confirmed with the tester that you have done all you need to do.

Date
Comments

Tester

Where to do your badge

Some parts of a badge are easier to do on holiday, at home or at school. If this is the case, make sure you get a note from the activity instructor, or your parent, guardian or teacher, saying you did it properly. Let them have a look at this book to check what you should be doing. If you complete a whole badge, ask them to sign the panel at the end of the badge.

Pick your style

For most badges you must show your skill at doing something, or show what you know about the subject. There are lots of ways you can do this, for example using a computer, acting, taking photographs or discussing with the tester. Pick an exciting way to show how you know things. Talk your ideas through with your Brownie Leader first.

Try it this way

You may not need to have everything checked. For some badges if you hold one of the certificates or awards listed you could get the badge. Check in the 'Try it this way' box with the badge to see if this option is given.

Need any help?

There is lots of help for you. Ask your Brownie Leaders for ideas of where to get help. Your parents or guardians, teachers or a local club can also help you.

Don't forget there are lots of books, magazines and websites that can be useful, too. If you use the internet, remember to use your Brownie web safe code (see page 8). Before making any phone calls check it is all right with the person who will pay the bill.

At the end of some badges are suggestions of where you may be able to get help.

My Brownie web safe code

When using the world wide web
I promise:

- to agree rules with my parents or guardians about the best way for me to use the computer and the world wide web.
- not to give out my home address or phone number without permission.
- not to give out the name or address of my school without permission.
- not to agree to meet anyone who I contact on the web, unless my parents or guardians say it is all right and go with me.
- not to put my photograph on a website.
- to tell my parents, guardians, teacher or Brownie Leader if I find something on the web that worries or upsets me.

With thanks to the Girl Scouts of the USA for the ideas contained within this warning for children.

To help you remember, this symbol has been put next to web addresses in this book.

Web safe

Got your badge

There are lots of ways you can show off your new badge. Take a look in your *Brownie Adventure* book for some exciting ideas.

Then it's time to decide if you want to try another one straight away, or wait for a bit.

Agility

Before doing any exercise you should warm up fully.
At the end, stretch out properly to cool down.

1 Do both of the following.
  - Warm up before taking exercise and stretch out afterwards.
  - Know about the clothes and equipment you need for the activities you choose.

2 Do one of the following.
  - Skip 60 steps forwards without a break.
  - Skip 20 steps backwards and show three fancy steps, for example a double-turn or a cross-over.
  - Spin a hoop around your waist for 20 seconds without a break.

3 Do one of the following.
  - Make up a one minute aerobic exercise sequence. Encourage other members of your Six to join in.
  - Take part in a three minute aerobic exercise sequence.

4 Follow a training circuit that has three of the following activities. Do each activity for 15 seconds.
  - Sit ups.
  - Balancing on one leg.
  - Running on the spot.
  - Hopping.
  - Press ups.
  - Tuck jumps.

5 Using two different balls, throw each ball against a wall ten times using both underarm and overarm throws. Catch each ball as it bounces back.

Date
Comments

Tester

Need any help?
British Gymnastics **Ford Hall, Lilleshall National Sports Centre, Newport, Shropshire, TF10 9NB**
0845 129 7129 www.british-gymnastics.org

Web safe

Tester tips
- The tester should be either a sports teacher or a suitably experienced adult.
- Clauses may be adapted to suit needs, and should remain challenging.

Try it this way
Practise for and take the test using the correct safety equipment (including floor mats) and under supervision.

Artist

1 Name the primary colours. Know how to mix them to make other colours.

2 Use three colours to make a pattern. Use any method you like, for example potato cuts, home-made stick prints or coloured paper. Suggest a suitable use for the pattern, such as wrapping paper or clothing.

3 Make two of the following.
  ● An invitation to celebrate a Brownie event.
  ● An illustrated poem, reading or prayer card.
  ● A picture using paints, crayons, inks or other colouring materials.
  ● A decorated bookmark.
  ● A greetings or thank-you card.
  ● A scented or textured picture.
  ● A piece of art designed on a computer.

4 Create a textured collage using materials like dried pasta, string and cloth.

5 At the test, draw or paint a picture of a subject you and the tester have agreed on before the test.

Date
Comments

Tester

Tester tips
● One item may be made at school.
● Clauses may be adapted to suit each Brownie's needs, and should remain challenging.
● A Brownie who has a visual impairment may prefer to create scented or textured pictures.

Try it this way
The different materials and techniques you can use are too long to list. Use your imagination.

Booklover

1 Make a list of four books that you have enjoyed. Discuss them with the tester.

2 With the tester choose two more books by different authors. When you have finished them, talk about them with the tester.

3 Show that you can care for a book, for example how to:
- cover a new book to keep it clean.
- use a book sleeve.
- place and remove a book from a shelf.
- store books.
- turn pages.

4 Make a bookmark for a friend or relative.

5 Show how to use a reference book, including the contents and index.

6 Know where your local library is and know its opening times. Make a poster showing some of the things you can borrow from the library.

Date
Comments

Tester

Need any help?
The librarian at your school or local library should be able to help you choose books.

Try it this way
You can pick poetry and fact books, as well as stories.

Tester tips
- Audiobooks, or books read aloud may be used for this badge.
- Choose reference books that are appropriate to the Brownie's age.

Brownie camper

1 Attend a Brownie camp from beginning to end.

2 Take part in a new activity with your Brownie friends at camp.

3 Do both of the following.
- Keep a diary when you are at camp. Tell another Brownie about the best things you did.
- Make something as a keepsake of your Brownie camp.

4 Do both of the following.
- Show how you would dress for wet weather and hot weather at camp.
- Know why it is important to keep yourself clean, warm and dry when at camp.

5 At camp help to:
- prepare and cook a meal.
- wash up and clear away afterwards.
- collect water and (if needed) wood.

6 Do both of the following.
- Show how to take care of your bedding during the day and how to keep it dry.
- Know why you should keep things away from the sides of the tent.

Date
Comments

Tester

Try it this way
- Your diary can include pictures or writing.
- Make a note in your diary of the funniest thing that happened, what you learned, the best thing that happened, your worst moment or what you liked best.
- Keep a record of the games and activities you did.
- You may want to tell friends who aren't Brownies about how much fun it was to go on Brownie camp.

Tester tips
- The tester does not have to hold a Brownie Camp Licence, but should be a Leader who takes part in the Brownie camp.
- The test can take place during the Brownie camp.

Brownie camper advanced

You don't have to have the Brownie camper badge before working for this badge.

1 Do both of the following.
- You should have spent at least four nights or more away at Brownie camp.
- Make a poster showing your favourite things about Brownie camp.

2 Help organise an activity with your Brownie friends at camp.

3 Tell a Brownie who has never been to camp what camp life is like. Help her learn the following camp skills.
- How to keep bedding and clothes dry.
- Keep the camp area safe and tidy.
- Prepare, cook and serve meals.
- Wash up and clear away after a meal.

4 Help another Brownie make something to remind her of the camp, or to keep a camp diary.

5 Help plan the camp, including:
- choosing the theme or reason for going.
- suggesting activities, games and places to visit.
- planning meals and menus.

6 Do all of the following.
- Know how to keep safe when you are out and about at Brownie camp.
- Know how to keep the camp area safe.
- Know the Country Code, the Green Cross Code and the Water Safety Code.

Date
Comments
Tester

Tester tips
- The four nights away at camp do not have to be at the same event.
- Brownies can camp with Brownies from other units, for example at a District event, or join a Guide camp with other Brownies.
- The tester does not have to hold a Brownie Camp Licence, but should be a Leader who takes part in the Brownie camp.
- The test can take place during the Brownie camp, and clause 6 can be done on a walk round the site.

Brownie holiday

1 Attend a Brownie holiday from beginning to end.

2 Take part in a new activity with your Brownie friends on holiday.

3 Do both of the following.
● Keep a diary when you are on holiday. Tell another Brownie about the best things you did.
● Make something as a keepsake of your Brownie holiday.

4 Know why it is important to keep healthy while on holiday.

5 On holiday help to:
● prepare and cook a meal.
● wash up and clear away afterwards.

6 Every day on holiday, make your bed and keep your things neat and tidy.

Date
Comments

Tester

Try it this way
● Your diary can include pictures or writing.
● Make a note in your diary of the funniest thing that happened, what you learned, the best thing that happened, your worst moment or what you liked best.
● Keep a record of the games and activities you did.
● You may want to tell friends who aren't Brownies about how much fun it was to go on Brownie holiday.

Tester tips
● The tester does not have to hold a Brownie Holiday Licence, but should be a Leader who takes part in the Brownie holiday.
● The test can take place during the Brownie holiday.

Brownie holiday advanced

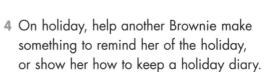

You don't have to have the Brownie holiday badge before working for this badge.

1 Do both of the following.
- You should have spent at least four nights or more away at Brownie holiday.
- Make a poster showing your favourite things about Brownie holiday.

2 Help organise an activity with your Brownie friends on holiday.

3 Tell a Brownie who has never been on holiday what holiday life is like. Help her learn the following holiday skills.
- Prepare, cook and serve meals on holiday.
- Wash up and clear away after a meal.
- Keep the holiday house safe and tidy.
- How to make a bed and keep belongings tidy.

4 On holiday, help another Brownie make something to remind her of the holiday, or show her how to keep a holiday diary.

5 Help plan the holiday, including:
- choosing the theme or reason for going.
- suggesting activities, games and places to visit.
- planning meals and menus.

6 Do all of the following.
- Know how to keep safe when you are out and about on Brownie holiday.
- Know how to keep the holiday house safe.
- Know the Country Code, the Green Cross Code and the Water Safety Code.

Date
Comments

Tester

Tester tips
- The four nights away on holiday do not have to be at the same event.
- Brownies can go on holiday with Brownies from other units, for example at a District event, or join a Guide holiday with other Brownies.
- The tester does not have to hold a Brownie Holiday Licence, but should be a Leader who takes part in the Brownie holiday.
- The test can take place during the Brownie holiday, and clause 6 can be done on a walk round the premises.

Brownie skills

Choose and do five of the following.

- Plan and make a healthy packed lunch. Know the types of food you should eat to keep healthy.
- Use a bus or train timetable to plan a journey.
- Sew on a button or a badge.
- Show how to read a simple map.
- Show how to wash and iron your Brownie clothes.
- Know what to do if there is a problem at home with the gas, electricity or water supply. Use a telephone directory to find the emergency numbers for each supplier.
- Help at an event where you have to collect money and give change.
- Show how you would pack a bag for a weekend away from home.

- Know how to keep yourself safe at home, in the town and in the country.
- Show how to wash your hands and clean your teeth properly. Know why it is important to do these things, and when you should do them.
- Show that you can address an envelope correctly. Explain to the tester why postcodes are important.
- Show how to tie two different knots. Know what each knot can be used for.

Date
Comments

Tester

Tester tips
A note from a parent, guardian or teacher is acceptable where appropriate.

Brownie traditions

1 Make a quiz or game, or put on a short play for other Brownies about all of the following.
- When Brownies started.
- What Brownies were first called.
- How Brownie uniform has changed.

2 Choose and do three of these traditional Brownie activities.
- Tie a reef knot and know when it can be used. Tie a bow in shoelaces. Make a single plait with thin rope or cord.
- Draw the Union flag and know how it is made up.
- Show how Brownies used to tie their scarf.
- Know the first verse of *The National Anthem*.
- Safely light a candle using a match.
- Find out what Brownies used to carry in their pockets.
- Find out about your Six emblem.
- With other Brownies, sing some of the Six songs that Brownies used to sing.
- Draw a Brownie First Class badge. Know what 'flying up' and 'gaining your wings' involved.
- Draw a picture of a Brownie magic carpet.
- Find out what the Brownie fitness exercise and Brownie health rules were. Do them both for a week.

3 Make a scrapbook or poster showing what you think Brownies will be doing in ten years.

Date
Comments

Tester

Need any help?
- Ask any of your Brownie Leaders what it was like when she was a Brownie. Does she still have her uniform or handbook that she can show you?
- Ask your local guiding archivist to show you any old Brownie materials she has.

Safety
Ask an adult you know for help when working with fire and matches.

Be safe

Circus performer

1 Learn two of the following circus skills.
 ● Juggling with three or more items, such as balls, rings, scarves or clubs.
 ● Plate-spinning.
 ● Yo-yo (show three tricks).
 ● Diabolo.
 ● Lasso.
 ● Stilt-walking.
 ● Tumbling and acrobatics.
 ● Unicycling.

2 Do one of the following.
 ● Make a set of juggling balls or bean bags.
 ● Perform your skills to a group, such as your Six or other Brownies.
 ● Try one other skill from the list of circus skills.

3 Visit a circus or circus skills workshop. Tell the tester about it.

4 Do both of the following.
 ● Paint a circus clown's face.
 ● Put on a short clown show.

Date
Comments

Tester

Tester tips
● The tester does not have to be someone with juggling or circus skills.
● This badge may be tested at a circus skills workshop where other suitable activities are being taught.

Need any help?
● Look in your phone book, library or newspaper for details of local circus skills workshops, classes and shops.
● The youth service department of your council may be able to help.

Collector

1 Make a collection to do with something that interests you, such as:
- postcards.
- badges.
- coins.
- stamps.

Arrange and, if necessary, label your items.

2 Tell the tester about your collection.
- How long you have had it.
- Where the items came from.
- What you like about it.
- Your favourite items.
- How you plan to extend it.

3 Choose and do one of the following.
- Know about the history of the items you collect.
- Know about a famous collection or collector of similar items.

4 Visit two other collections, for example at a museum, art gallery, zoo or library. Describe your visits and how the collections were displayed.

Date

Comments

Tester

Tester tips
The tester does not need to be an expert in the items being collected.

Try it this way
If you have another collection, you can work for this badge again.

Need any help?
Search for websites that are relevant to your collection.

Web safe

19

Communicator

Choose and do three of the following. Discuss with and show the tester what you've done.

- Act or mime a scene from a recent Brownie event you have attended.
- Take part in World Thinking Day on the Air, or another special amateur radio event.
- Know how two-way radios, such as those used by the police, ships and aeroplanes, can be useful.
- Be able to spell your name and home town using the phonetic alphabet (A = Alpha, B = Bravo, C = Charlie and so on).
- Write or dictate a reading, poem or prayer then read it aloud.
- Learn the finger-spelling alphabet or other recognised non-verbal communication and be able to:
  - 'say' your name.
  - ask someone their name and understand the reply.

- In a language other than your own:
  - say your name.
  - order some food and drink.
  - count to ten.
  - say hello and goodbye.
- Pass on a message clearly using a phone. Show how to use a payphone or a mobile phone.
- Show five types of body language, for example feeling happy, sad, angry, fed up or confused.
- Make a poster, audio-recorded or video-recorded advert for Brownies.
- Send an email or letter to the tester saying what you would like to do on Brownie camp or holiday, and what you enjoy about Brownies.
- Using your Brownie web safe code, take part in a live web event, such as World Thinking Day on the Internet.

Web safe

Date
Comments

Tester

Try it this way
If you complete three more clauses you may have another Communicator badge.

Computer

1 Show how to do all of the following.
- Turn on a computer.
- Start a programme you want to use.
- Use a mouse, joystick or graphics tablet.
- Handle CDs to keep them clean.
- Save something you have created to the hard drive or to a CD.
- Print your work.
- Shut down the computer when you've finished.

2 Know what a computer virus is and how to prevent being affected by one.

3 Choose and do one of the following.
- Write a letter or story using a word-processing programme. Use a range of fonts and sizes. If possible use colours and insert pictures or clip art. Save it and print it out.
- Use a graphics package to create a piece of art. Save it and print it out.
- Download images from a digital camera or scan printed photographs. Use the images to create a photodiary of a Brownie event you have attended.

4 Do all of the following.
- Know the importance of the Brownie web safe code and show that you follow it when using the web.
- Log on to the Internet and visit www.girlguiding.org.uk. Find out two facts about Brownies and email them to the tester.
- With the tester, visit two websites. Explain which is your favourite one. Save the site on your bookmark.

5 Use a search engine to find out about one of the following.
- Your favourite pop star.
- A historical figure.
- A sport you are interested in.
- A country you would like to visit.

Date
Comments

Tester

Need any help?
Take a look at the Brownie web safe code on page 8 of this book.

Web safe

Cook

1 Do all of the following.
- Show how to handle kitchen utensils safely. These should include knives and scissors.
- Show and explain how to be safe in the kitchen.
- Explain the basics of food hygiene.

2 Choose and do two of the following.
- Make breakfast for three or four other people that includes two of these dishes.
  - Toast with jam or marmalade.
  - A dish using eggs.
  - A simple cooked breakfast, such as beans on toast.
  - Porridge.
  - A muesli mix you have created.
  - Tea or coffee.
  - Freshly squeezed fruit juice.
  - Any other dish you usually eat for breakfast.
- Make a healthy dish showing you can prepare fresh fruits, vegetables or salad. Arrange it in an appetising way.
- Bake and decorate biscuits, cakes or scones. Share them with other Brownies.
- Make a simple lunch snack for yourself and someone else.

3 Wash up and clear away after a meal.

Date
Comments

Tester

Need any help?
- There are lots of cookery programmes on TV which may give you ideas.
- Visit www.5aday.nhs.uk for hints and tips.

Web safe

Try it this way
- This badge can be done with friends, or on Brownie holiday.
- One of the dishes may be prepared at school.

Tester tips
A note from a parent, guardian or teacher is acceptable where appropriate.

Cook advanced

You don't have to have the Cook badge before working for this badge.

1 Do all of the following.
- Show how to handle sharp knives, scissors and other kitchen utensils safely.
- Show and explain how to improve safety in the kitchen.
- Explain the basics of food hygiene and how to store foods correctly.

2 Prepare a simple two-course meal: one course must be cooked.

3 Choose and do one of the following.
- Make a poster for your meeting place, school or Brownie holiday that illustrates one of the following.
  - Food allergies.
  - Healthy eating.
  - The different food groups.
  - The countries that different foods come from.
- Make a collection of the recipes you have most enjoyed trying. Make sure your collection includes savoury and sweet dishes.

4 Show how to do two of the following.
- Use a dishwasher.
- Clean and care for non-stick cookware.
- Wash up in the correct order.
- Clean a microwave oven.
- Clean a fridge.

5 Do one of the following.
- Prepare a traditional dish from another country.
- Plan and prepare the food for a Rainbow party or children's birthday party.
- Prepare a dish using an ingredient you've never used before.
- With an adult you know, cook a meal outdoors on a stove or barbecue.

Be safe

Need any help?
- There are lots of cookery programmes on TV which may give you ideas.
- Visit www.5aday.nhs.uk for hints and tips.

Web safe

Tester tips
A note from a parent, guardian or teacher is acceptable where appropriate.

Date
Comments
Tester

Try it this way
- This badge can be done with friends or on Brownie holiday.
- One of the dishes may be prepared at school.

Craft

Choose and do three of the following. Finish two of them to show the tester. Explain how you made them and what you will do with them. Take the third item to the test unfinished to show the tester how you will finish it.

- Make a bag or t-shirt decorated with printing or dyeing.
- Use a papercraft, like marbling, paper making, quilling or origami, to create something decorative.
- Weave an item, for example a friendship bracelet or coaster.
- Create a scented or textured collage using a variety of materials, such as cloth, paper, felt, wool, natural objects, dried pastas and pulses.
- Make a piñata or other useful item using papier mâché.
- Create an ornament from natural materials, such as wood or stone.
- Design and make a garden in a box or bottle.
- Design a garden using a computer programme. Print out your design.
- Design your ideal bedroom using pictures from catalogues, paint, wallpaper and fabric samples. You can use a computer design programme.
- Make two matching items of jewellery from home-made beads or pendants.
- Knit something that would be useful, such as a scarf, cushion or item of clothing for a baby or child.
- Sew, by hand or using a machine, a useful item, such as a book mark or pencil case. Decorate it with embroidery stitches.
- Decorate a mirror or suncatcher with glass paints.
- Make an item using a craft from another country or from your local area.
- Create something using a craft technique of your choice.

Date
Comments

Tester

Tester tips
- One item for each badge may be made at school.
- Clauses may be adapted to suit each Brownie's needs, and should remain challenging.
- Brownies with a visual impairment may prefer to create scented or textured items.

Try it this way
- The different materials and techniques you can use are too long to list. Use your imagination.
- If you complete three more clauses you can have another Craft badge.

Crime prevention

1 Do both of the following.
  - Know what to tell your parents or guardians before going out without them.
  - Know what to do if a stranger talks to you.

2 Make a poster to encourage children not to damage other people's property.

3 Do both of the following.
  - Show how property-marking schemes that use the postcode can work.
  - Know how to keep your possessions safe when you are out and about.

4 Do both of the following.
  - Get two leaflets about crime prevention from your local police station or crime prevention officer. Discuss the messages with the tester.
  - Find out about two property protection schemes, such as the Neighbourhood Watch Scheme or Home Watch Scheme. Draw the signs used to show where these schemes are happening.

5 Explain how to protect your home from burglary when everyone from your home:
  - goes out for the whole day or for part of the day.
  - is away overnight or on holiday.

6 Act out a short play with your Six showing how you would keep yourself safe.

Date
Comments

Tester

Need any help?
- **Ask your local police or crime prevention officer for help and advice.**
- **Visit www.neighbourhoodwatch.net for ideas.**

Web safe

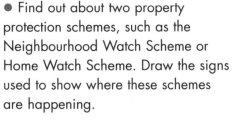

Culture

Choose and do three of the following.

- Make a collection of items to reflect your everyday life. This could include photos, maps, your favourite clothes or food, what you do at Brownies and so on. Show it to your Six and the tester before storing it somewhere safe to open in the future.
- Draw a family tree in a way that looks nice.
- Learn a song, poem, dance or story from the area where you live, or from your own culture. Teach it to your Six.
- Find out about the history of your Pack:
    - how long it has been running.
    - talk with older members you know.
    Share what you discover with your Six or other Brownies.

- Make a dish that is traditional to your local area or culture. Share it with other Brownies.
- Talk about how people's cultures affect their lifestyles.
- Hold a party for your Six to celebrate in a traditional way a birthday or festival that is important to you.
- Visit your local museum to find out about some of the collections and exhibits.
- Talk with an adult you know about how the area where you live has changed.

Date
Comments

Tester

Try it this way
- You could draw the family tree of a famous family.
- If you complete three more clauses you can have another Culture badge.

Tester tips
One item for each badge may be made at school.

26

Cyclist

When riding a bicycle you must wear a helmet that fits you and is not damaged.

1 Show how to check that a bicycle is safe to ride. Show how to check that the chain, brakes and tyres are all in good order.

2 Do all of the following.
- Wear clothing that is safe for cycling.
- Explain why it is important to be seen when cycling.
- Know where to find details of the lighting-up time. Show how to keep lights and reflectors in working order.

3 Make a simple repair kit to carry with you when cycling. Bring it to the test and show how to use the items.

4 In a safe area, safely ride your bicycle:
- in and out of a line of blocks or cones.
- using the brakes correctly.

5 Go cycling with the tester or an adult you know. Show that you understand:
- the Highway Code for cyclists.
- hand signals that cyclists use.
- how to carry essential items.

Be safe

Date
Comments

Tester

Try it this way
You can be tested for this badge on a borrowed bicycle that is the right size for you and is in good working order.

Need any help?
- Most cycling clubs have a junior section that you can join.
- Visit www.bikeability.org.uk/kids for safe cycling information.

Web safe

Dancer

1 Choose and do one of the following.
- Make a collection about three of your favourite types of dance. You could include:
  - pictures.
  - music.
  - information on the costumes worn.
  - details of famous dancers.
  - history.
- Know the stories of three well-known ballets.
- Find out about the national dances of three countries, including their history, the costumes worn and the music played as an accompaniment.

2 Complete one of the following sections. Talk with the tester about the dances you do.

Folk and national dance
Know three dances and be able to perform them really well.

Creative dance
Do both of the following.
- Use one of the following ideas to make up a simple dance.
  - Tell a well-known story.
  - Interpret a picture.
  - Make a pattern.
You can dance with or without sound.
- Perform a simple dance to one of these:
  - a rhythm played on a percussion instrument.
  - a piece of music you have brought with you.

Ballet
You should hold the Grade 1 Certificate from a teaching society recognised by the Council for Dance Education and Training or any other recognised equivalent certificate. At the test perform a dance lasting one minute using the steps in that grade.

Wheelchair dancing

Perform three dances of different character in a self-propelled or assisted wheelchair.

Other forms of dance

Hold the First Grade Certificate or Bronze Medal of the nationally-recognised dance organisation for that dance form, such as tap, Greek, ballroom and so on.

Date
Comments

Tester

Need any help?
There are many recognised forms of dance. For more information contact Council for Dance Education and Training Old Brewer's Yard, 17–19 Neal Street, London, WC2H 9UY 020 7240 5703 www.cdet.org.uk

Web safe

Try it this way
If you complete different options from both clauses you can have another Dancer badge.

Tester tips
The tester will look for correct movements as well as how you express yourself through dance.

Designer

1 Choose four items from the list below. Create a design for each item, remembering that you need to be able to:

- explain how and why you came up with your idea.
- show the tester your original ideas, as well as your final design.
- explain your choice of materials.

Design ideas

- An outfit you could wear on holiday.
- Something useful made by recycling materials.
- An advert for Brownies, such as for a billboard, in a magazine, on a website, on the television or on the radio.
- A cover for your favourite book.
- Something to make an elderly person's life easier.
- A web page.
- A garden, window box or patio.
- A gadget for the future.
- A badge for a special event.

2 Find out something about a famous designer. Tell your Six about the designer in an interesting way, using pictures of their work.

Date
Comments

Tester

Disability awareness

1 Choose and do two clauses from each section.

Mobility awareness

● Talk with the tester about mobility aids, such as powered and manual wheelchairs, walking frames and canes. Know when they may be useful.

● Know three ways to make it easier for a wheelchair-user to use public places, like shops, parks, hospitals or libraries. Describe how your meeting place could be improved for a wheelchair-user.

● Make a poster or leaflet showing some of the events that form the Paralympics.

● Make up, or change, a game or activity so that everyone can take part in it, however mobile they are.

Deaf awareness

There are two types of deafness:
● pre-lingual deafness, where a person is deaf from birth.
● acquired deafness, where a person becomes deaf.

● Learn the finger-spelling alphabet. Use it to:
  – tell the tester your name.
  – find out the tester's name.

● Explain what hearing dogs for deaf people do and why they are helpful.

● Take part in a game or activity at Brownies wearing earplugs or headphones so you can't hear clearly. Describe how you felt.

● Show how to:
  – approach a deaf person.
  – speak to a deaf person so they can lip-read.

Sight awareness

- Find out about the different ways a blind or visually-impaired person can read, for example using the computer, Braille or Moon.
- Explain what guide dogs for blind people do and how they are trained.
- With your eyes closed, identify:
  - four objects by touch.
  - four objects by sound.
  - four objects by smell.
- Show how to approach and identify yourself to a blind or visually-impaired person.

2 Find out about two other disabilities. Know how they can affect someone's life.

Date
Comments
Tester

Need any help?

Deaf awareness

- **For an information pack contact the** Royal National Institute for Deaf People (RNID) **19–23 Featherstone Street, London, EC1Y 8SL textphone 0808 808 9000 (free) telephone 0808 808 0123 (free) email information@rnid.org.uk** www.rnid.org.uk
- **A finger-spelling alphabet can be found in** *Brownies Adventure On*, **or visit** www.britishsignlanguage.com

Sight awareness

Royal National Institute of Blind People (RNIB) **105 Judd Street, London, WC1H 9NE 020 7388 1266** www.rnib.org.uk

Mobility awareness

Whizz-Kidz **Elliot House, 10–12 Allington Street, London, SW1E 5EH 020 7233 6600** www.whizz-kidz.org.uk

Web safe

Try it this way

If you complete the other options from each section in clause 1, and find out about another two disabilities for clause 2, you can have a second Disability awareness badge.

Discovering faith

1 Regularly go to a place where you can learn about a faith. This could be a church (mid-week club or Sunday school), gurdwara, mosque, synagogue, temple or other place of worship.

2 Choose and do one of the following.
● Take part in a Brownie's Own or Thought for the Moment with other Brownies. Use songs, stories, drama, mime or music, with at least one piece being from your own faith.
● Write a prayer or poem about keeping your Brownie Promise. Use it at a suitable event.

3 Find out about someone whose faith plays an important part in the way they live their life.

4 Do both of the following.
● Find out about a religiously-based organisation that works for the good of other people, like Christian Aid, Khalsa Aid, SEWA International, Muslim Aid or Jewish Care. Make a poster about their activities.
● Describe a good turn you have done. Explain how it helped you to understand your Brownie Promise.

5 Find out about at least two festivals or celebrations from your own faith or another. Make a poster or collage, take photographs or write a story or poem about one of them.

6 Find out how local communities have enjoyed themselves together, for example at a joint Brownie and Cub event or an inter-faith celebration.

Date
Comments

Tester

Try it this way
Find out about your chosen person by reading a book, watching a TV programme or video, or listening to a radio programme. The person you choose may be someone from the past or who is living now.

Tester tips
A Brownie does not have to follow one particular faith to work for this badge. She must be interested in finding out how faith is important to people's lives.

Entertainer

1 Choose and plan an entertainment doing three of the following.
- Recite a poem or tell a short story.
- Act, mime or use puppets to tell the story of an historical event.
- Perform a national dance or create your own dance to music.
- Sing with or without accompaniment.
- Play a piece on a musical instrument.
- Perform a short magic show.
- Act as compère for a show put on by other Brownies who are working for their Entertainer badge.

2 Do both of the following.
- Rehearse for your show. Plan make-up, costume and lighting.
- Make a programme for the event.

3 Entertain an audience and clear up afterwards.

Date
Comments

Tester

Need any help?
- **Look in your local library or newspaper for details of drama groups.**
- **If you have a drama teacher at school, ask them for some advice.**

Try it this way
If you complete three more choices from clause 1 and complete clauses 2 and 3 you can have a second Entertainer badge.

Tester tips
- **A small group of Brownies may work for this badge together, but each Brownie must perform at least one item on her own.**
- **The audience can be other Brownies.**

Environment

1 Do both of the following.
- For a week, try three different ways to use less water and energy at home.
- Keep a record of what you've done and how much less water and energy you have used.

2 Do both of the following.
- Collect packaging that can and cannot be recycled. Know how you would:
  - dispose of each item safely.
  - reduce packaging waste.
- Show how you sort items in to recycling groups and where your local recycling facilities are found.

3 Find out about your local recycling facilities. Make a poster showing what can be recycled and where the collection points are for at least three different materials.

4 Do one of the following.
- Visit a local farmers' market and find out why buying produce there helps the farmer, you and the environment.
- Collect six food items, such as apples, pineapples or coffee. Discuss whether they are produced in this country or another. Know the issues with transporting food a long way.

5 Explain how artificial fertilisers, pesticides and the destruction of hedgerows affect wildlife.

6 Find out about an endangered species, like red squirrels, tigers, blue whales or giant pandas. Make a display or information pack about them.

Date

Comments

Tester

Need any help?
- Look in your local library or contact your council for details about local recycling facilities.
- These organisations can provide information about endangered animals:
  - WWF-UK Panda House, Weyside Park, Godalming, Surrey, GU7 1XR 01483 426444 www.wwf.org.uk
  - World Society for the Protection of Animals (WSPA) 89 Albert Embankment, London, SE1 7TP 020 7587 5000 or visit www.wspa.org.uk

Try it this way
- Keep a scrapbook with all your water and energy conservation records.
- Look at the food labels in your kitchen, or when visiting the supermarket, to see where foods come from.

Web safe

Finding your way

1 Do all of the following.
- Describe the easiest and quickest way of getting from your meeting place to local shops or a shopping centre.
- Know the best way of getting to two nearby towns, villages or shopping centres.
- Know suitable routes for someone using a wheelchair or pushing a pram.

2 Give clear directions on how to get to some local places from your Brownie meeting place. For example:
- the post office.
- police station.
- library.
- place of worship.
- hospital.
- community centre.
- school.
- local shop.

Draw a map for a new Brownie showing some of these places and your meeting place.

3 Take the tester to a nearby building or landmark following directions you have been given. You may use a simple map of the area, follow signs or look for landmarks.

4 Describe your local bus, train or tram services. Know where to catch these services and when they run.

5 Do both of the following.
- Act out a short play about being safe when out and about.
- Know about the Green Cross Code, the Country Code and the Water Safety Code.

6 Tell the tester what you know about stranger danger.

| Date |
| Comments |
| |
| Tester |

Try it this way
When practising for this badge go out with an adult you know, or a group of friends.

Be safe

Tester tips
- The tester must be known to the Brownie.
- The routes may use public transport.

Need any help?
A map of your local area may be available from your local stationer or newsagent.

Fire safety

1 Find out how the fire service works and what happens when it receives an emergency call.

2 Know how most fires in the home start. Talk with the tester about some ways to prevent fires from starting.

3 Know about battery-operated and hard-wired smoke detectors. Describe:
● the best places to put smoke detectors.
● the sound a smoke detector makes.
● how and when to test smoke detectors.

4 Make an escape plan for your home or meeting place. You should include:
● two ways out of each room (if possible).
● a meeting point outside, where everyone should go to.
Make sure everyone knows how to get out if there is a fire. Practise your escape plan at least once.

5 Describe each of the following.
● How to call the fire service in an emergency.
● How to escape from a room filled with smoke.
● How to prevent smoke entering a room.
● How to check for fire behind a door, knowing not to open it if there is fire.
● What you would do if your own (or someone else's) clothes caught fire.

6 Describe basic fire safety for:
● ovens, hobs, grills, microwave ovens and toasters.
● fires and heaters.
● people who smoke.

Date

Comments

Tester

Need any help?
● Contact your local fire station for information on fire safety, or invite a fire officer to your meeting.
● Children's Fire and Burn Trust
38 Buckingham Palace Road, London, SW1W ORE 020 7233 8333
www.childrensfireandburntrust.org.uk
or www.welephant.co.uk

Tester tips
The tester should be qualified in fire safety.

Web safe

37

First aid

1 Discuss with the tester:
- why first aid is important.
- why you should get medical help as soon as possible and how you would do this.
- why you should get adult help as soon as possible.
- why you must think of your own safety before rushing to help a casualty.
- how you think someone might feel if they have had an accident.

2 Do all of the following.
- Know how to check whether a casualty is unconscious or not.
- Show how to open an airway.
- Show how to check someone for normal breathing.
- Show how to put a casualty in the recovery position. Explain when and why you would do this.

3 Do both of the following.
- Know why your blood is important to you. Show how you would deal with the following types of bleeding.
  - Small graze or cut.
  - Nosebleed.
  - Serious deep cut with a lot of bleeding.
  - Cut that has a piece of glass in it.
- Explain how and why you would protect yourself when dealing with a casualty who is bleeding.

4 Know what causes burns and scalds. Show how you would treat them.

5 Do both of the following.
- Describe what would make you suspect that someone had a broken bone.
- Show what you would do if you thought a bone was broken.

Date

Comments

Tester

38

Tester tips

● It is important that anyone teaching or testing this badge has a current full first aid qualification and is using protocols from the current edition of a recognised first aid manual.

● The initial discussion on accidents and injuries in clause 1 should show if a Brownie is ready and mature enough to complete this badge. The other clauses should only be completed by a Brownie who the tester thinks could carry out the procedures safely in a real situation.

● The tester must be sure that a Brownie understands the importance of DRAB and how to manage an incident: this can be done as a group scenario provided that each Brownie also shows an understanding of all parts of each clause.

Need any help?

● **British Red Cross** UK Office, **44 Moorfields, London, EC2Y 9AL 0844 871 11 11** www.redcross.org.uk

● St Andrew's First Aid **St Andrew's House, 48 Milton Street, Glasgow, G4 0HR 0141 332 4031** www.firstaid.org.uk

● **St John Ambulance 27 St John's Lane, London, EC1M 4BU 08700 10 49 50** www.sja.org.uk

Web safe

Try it this way

● The tester will check to make sure you keep the casualty reassured and comfortable all the time.

39

First aid advanced

1 Hold the First aid badge.

2 Do both of the following.
- Use a resuscitation manikin to show how to give chest compressions followed by rescue breaths.
- Know when you might need to do this and how to carry it out safely.

3 Discuss with the tester:
- what shock is.
- why someone who has had a serious accident may suffer shock.
- how to recognise shock.
- why it is important to deal with shock quickly.

Date

Comments

Tester

Tester tips
- It is important that anyone teaching or testing this badge has a current full first aid qualification and is using protocols from the current edition of a recognised first aid manual.
- By completing the First aid badge (pages 38–39) a Brownie should show that she is ready and mature enough to complete this badge. The Brownie should be physically able to undertake CPR, as well as understand the importance of practising only on a resuscitation manikin and carrying out the procedure correctly in a real situation.
- The tester must be sure that a Brownie understands the importance of DRAB and how to manage an incident: this can be done as a group scenario provided each Brownie also shows an understanding of all parts of each clause.

Try it this way
The tester will check to make sure you keep the casualty reassured and comfortable all the time. If you hold one of the following certificates, you may have this badge:
- St John Ambulance Young Lifesaver Award Scheme Key Stage 2 (Junior).
- St Andrew's First Aid Junior Preliminary First Aid Certificate.

Need any help?
- British Red Cross UK Office, 44 Moorfields, London, EC2Y 9AL 0844 871 11 11 www.redcross.org.uk
- St Andrew's First Aid St Andrew's House, 48 Milton Street, Glasgow, G4 0HR 0141 332 4031 www.firstaid.org.uk
- St John Ambulance 27 St John's Lane, London, EC1M 4BU 08700 10 49 50 www.sja.org.uk

Web safe

Friend to animals

Either

Choose and do one clause from each section.

Or

Do all the clauses from one section.

Pets

- Make a poster or leaflet about your favourite pet animal showing:
  - what it eats.
  - where it comes from.
  - what kind of exercise it needs.
  - how it likes to play.
- Find out about working animals, like guide dogs or horses. Explain how they are trained and why they are useful.
- Choose an animal charity and find out about its work. Help support its work, for example join one of its sponsored events.
- Draw a picture or write a poem or story about a pet. Show what makes it special and individual.

Endangered animals

- Make a poster or leaflet about an endangered animal. Include details about:
  - where it lives.
  - what it eats.
  - why it is endangered.
- Choose a charity or organisation that helps protect endangered animals. Help support its work, for example join one of its sponsored events.
- Find out about some animals that are already extinct. Explain why this has happened, and what can be done so it doesn't happen in the future.
- Make up a quiz, game or activity about endangered animals for your Six.

Zoos, animal sanctuaries and wildlife reserves

- Visit your nearest zoo, animal sanctuary or wildlife reserve. Find out about some of the animals that live there, including at least one you hadn't heard of before. Make a scrapbook about your visit.
- Look at the different colours and patterns of animals. Explain why animals need camouflage. Use some of the patterns you see in a piece of art, for example a face mask.
- Describe how life is different for animals that live in the wild to those that live in captivity.
- Find out how some zoos' conservation work helps to protect endangered animals. Get details of the adoption schemes that are run by some zoos and sanctuaries.

Animal care

- Know why humans are a threat to animals, and what can be done about it. Make a poster or leaflet showing how Brownies can help.
- Imitate five animals for the rest of your Six to guess.
- Know where your local vet's surgery is and when it is open. Explain:
  - why your pet might need to visit the vet.
  - what you would do if you found a sick or stray animal.

- Make a book about animals for a young child. Choose at least five animals and say where they live, what they eat and what their babies are called.

Date

Comments

Tester

Need any help?

These organisations all help animals.

- The Blue Cross Shilton Road, Burford, Oxfordshire, OX18 4PF 01993 822651 www.bluecross.org.uk
- Cats Protection National Cat Centre, Chelwood Gate, Haywards Heath, Sussex, RH17 7TT 08702 099 099 www.cats.org.uk
- Dogs Trust 17 Wakley Street, London, EC1V 7RQ 020 7837 0006 www.dogstrust.org.uk
- People's Dispensary for Sick Animals (PDSA) Whitechapel Way, Priorslee, Telford, Shropshire, TF2 9PQ 01952 290999 www.pdsa.org.uk
- The Royal Society for the Prevention of Cruelty to Animals (RSPCA) Wilberforce Way, Southwater, Horsham, West Sussex, RH13 9RS 0300 1234 999 www.rspca.org.uk
- WWF-UK Panda House, Weyside Park, Godalming, Surrey, GU7 1XR 01483 426444 www.wwf.org.uk
- World Society for the Protection of Animals (WSPA) 89 Albert Embankment, London, SE1 7TP 020 7587 5000 www.wspa.org.uk

Web safe

Try it this way

- If possible, meet a working animal and its owner.
- If possible, visit an animal charity or rescue centre to find out what it does.
- If you complete a different option from each section, or another complete section, you can have another Friend to animals badge.

Safety

Remember, it is important to wash your hands after handling animals.

Be safe

Gardener

1 Explain how and why you keep your garden tidy and free from weeds.

2 Grow four kinds of fruits, vegetables, herbs or annual flowers from seed or bulb. Transplant the seedlings then tend and train them as necessary. Discuss with the tester how you will use what you have grown.

3 Do all of the following.
  ● Show which tools you use to care for your garden and how you keep them in good condition.
  ● Know the dangers of tools left lying around.
  ● Know the dangers of garden products, such as weedkillers.

4 Know how the following affect your garden.
  ● Light and shade.
  ● Temperature and weather conditions.
  ● Soil types.

Date
Comments

Tester

Try it this way
● Your garden may be an area in a larger garden or allotment, a window box, or a container garden in a courtyard or lobby.
● Be aware of the time of year and how this will affect the plants you can grow.

Tester tips
This badge can be tested over a period of time.

Safety
Remember, it is important to wash your hands after gardening.

Be safe

Need any help?
Visit these websites for some inspiration.
● www.bbc.co.uk/gardening
● www.chestnut-sw.com
● www.gardenorganic.org.uk

Web safe

Healthy heart

1 Know the three things that you need to do to keep your heart healthy.

2 Choose and do two clauses from each section.

Eating a healthy diet

● Make a poster that shows which foods are good and bad for your heart. Put it up in your meeting place, local library or doctor's surgery.

● Plan and prepare a healthy packed lunch.

● Keep a food diary for one week. Talk with the tester about how you could eat more healthily.

● Use food packaging to create a collage of the Balance of Good Health model showing the five food groups.

Being active

● Know how much exercise you should do each day to keep your heart healthy. Tell the tester your top ten activities for making your heart beat faster.

● Take your pulse before and after three different physical activities. Rest between each activity to let your heart rate return to normal. Know why this is good for your heart.

● Make a chart to show how much exercise you do each day for a week. Talk with the tester about whether you should change the type or amount of exercise you do.

● Make up a game to play with others at Brownies that will make your hearts beat faster.

Looking after your body

● Write a poem or song, or make a poster, about the damage caused by smoking.

● Find out about asthma. Know what to do if someone has an asthma attack.

● Explain why it is important to follow the instruction label on medicines carefully. Know how to dispose of medicines and pills safely.

● Know which foods most often cause allergic reactions. Know what someone who has a food allergy should do to keep healthy.

Date
Comments

Tester

Need any help?

● For more information about your heart and for a support pack for this badge, contact Heart Research UK Suite 12D, Joseph's Well, Leeds, West Yorkshire, LS3 1AB 0113 234 7474 www.heartresearch.org.uk

● Your local pharmacist or doctor's surgery may be able to help with information or leaflets.

● Some useful websites are:
  – www.nutrition.org.uk for 'Make a balanced plate' activity.
  – www.asthma.org.uk for information about asthma.
  – www.anaphylaxis.org.uk for information about allergies.

Web safe

Hobbies

1 For at least four weeks keep a diary about your hobby showing:
- how you have been involved.
- what you have done in your hobby.

2 Make a display about your hobby showing the following.
- What your hobby is.
- How you got involved.
- Why you enjoy it.
- What it involves, for example is there a club or are there any rules?
- How you could share your hobby with others.

3 Explain how someone could start doing your hobby. Try to include the cost, space, time and equipment needed.

4 Discuss with the tester what you have learned from your hobby and how you plan to develop it in the future.

Date

Comments

Tester

Try it this way
- Hobbies can involve a wide range of interests, such as bellringing, listening to music, photography, skiing or snorkelling.
- Your display could include photographs, pictures and other items to do with your hobby, like certificates and badges.
- If you have another hobby, you can work for this badge again.

Tester tips
The tester need not have any prior knowledge of the hobby.

Home safety

1 Do both of the following.
- Show how to do the following safely.
  - Make a hot drink.
  - Switch an electrical appliance on and off, such as a hairdryer, TV or CD-player.
- Know how to fill a bath safely.

2 Do both of the following.
- Study a room in your house looking for possible dangers. Draw a picture of the room showing the dangers. Think about the following.
  - Electrical sockets and plugs.
  - Trailing and damaged wires.
  - Clothes.
  - Toys.
  - Electrical equipment.
  - Windows.
  - Doors.
  - Furniture.
  - Floor coverings.
- Explain why you think they may be dangerous and how to make the room safer. Know what needs to be done, and who should do it.

3 Do both of the following.
- Make up a game or activity to help other Brownies learn how the following could be a danger to young children.
  - Plastic bags.
  - Medicines and pills left within reach.
  - Scissors, knives, needles and pins.
  - Chemicals like cleaning fluids and disinfectants.
- Know how to reduce these dangers.

4 Explain how and when to call the emergency services. Know how to use a household, mobile and public telephone in an emergency.

5 Do all of the following.
- Give the name, address and telephone number of a relative or neighbour who could help in an emergency.
- Know where there is a working torch for use in an emergency, for example in a power cut.
- Know how to contact your family doctor in an emergency.

Try it this way

When looking for things that may be unsafe in a room, remember they can be things that are easy to put right like tidying away toys, or may need adult help such as fitting a smoke alarm.

Date

Comments

Tester

Home skills

1 Clean two of the following.
- A window or mirror.
- A basin or sink.
- A cupboard or drawer.
- A pair of shoes.
- A car, inside or out.

2 Make your bed every day for a week. Tidy, dust and vacuum your bedroom.

3 Do all of the following.
- Explain what clothes care symbols mean.
- Show how you wash, dry and iron clothes.
- Describe the shaped colour-coded buttons used by visually-impaired or blind people.

4 Lay a table for a main meal. Wash up and clear away afterwards.

5 Make up a game or activity about recycling symbols on packaging. Discuss with the tester how you can improve recycling in your home.

Date
Comments

Tester

Tester tips
- A note from a parent or guardian is acceptable where appropriate.
- The test can take place during a Brownie holiday.

Hostess

1 Make an invitation for a friend asking them to come to tea, a party or a sleepover. Address the envelope correctly and know which stamp to use.

2 Make a plan showing:
- how many people you are expecting.
- when they should arrive.
- what refreshments you will serve them.
- the entertainment you will put on, such as a game, activity or small show.

3 Decorate a room or make a table decoration. Prepare refreshments for your guests.

4 Welcome and look after your guests. Serve them refreshments and entertain them.

5 Wash up and clear away afterwards.

Date
Comments

Tester

Try it this way
- You may design your invitation and plan using a computer programme.
- If you are planning to hold a party at home, make sure your parents or guardians are happy with all your plans first.

Tester tips
- Clauses can be completed with a friend, or a small group of Brownies may work for this badge together, but each Brownie must play a full role in both the planning and the event.
- The guests can be other Brownies or the tester.

Musician

1 Play or sing two contrasting pieces.

2 Choose and do one of the following.
- Sing or play at sight a simple piece and clap a rhythm.
- Make a percussion instrument and use it to accompany a well-known tune or song.

3 Take along some of your favourite music to listen to and discuss with the tester.

4 Show that you can:
- name different values of musical notes.
- name the notes on a stave.
- understand simple Italian musical terms.

Date
Comments

Tester

Try it this way
- If you play another instrument, you can work for this badge again.

Tester tips
- The tester should be a music teacher, or musician, who has knowledge of the instrument being played.
- The music for sight-reading should be of an appropriate level of difficulty.

Number fun

Choose and do five of the following.

- Imagine you have £500 to redesign your bedroom. Find out what kind of things you could buy and make a list to show how you would use the money.
- Help at an event where you have to collect money and give change.
- Keep a record of the money you are given and spend during one month.
- Find out about three types of money not used in your country. Know what the money is called, and which countries it is used in. If possible, have examples of the money to show others.
- Know how to open a savings account at a bank or building society. Find out about one savings account.
- Design a game that involves using money or that helps young children learn how to count.

- Make a birthday or address book. Use it to record at least ten people's details.
- Find out about different postage costs. Show that you can select the right stamps needed for an item.
- Carry out a survey of at least 20 people and share the results with the tester. The survey must include at least five questions.
- Show that you can tell the time using the 24-hour clock.
- Make up a number code. Use it to pass on a secret message.
- Plan a simple meal. Work out how much it would cost to buy the ingredients.

Date
Comments

Tester

Out and about

1 Show how to dress for walking and rambling. Pack a bag or daysack.

2 With an adult you know, go for a walk lasting at least 30 minutes and show:
- how to use a simple map of the area.
- how to set a map using landmarks.
- that you understand the Green Cross Code, Country Code and Water Safety Code.

Be safe

3 Choose and do one of the following.
- Plan and carry out a treasure hunt or scavenger hunt for your Six and the tester.
- Take part in a mini-hike or orienteering game.

4 Know what precautions you can take against bad weather and being caught in darkness.

5 Make a poster or act out a short play about keeping safe when out and about, for example how to be visible after dark or in the fog, stranger danger and so on.

Date
Comments

Tester

Try it this way
When preparing for this badge go out with an adult you know, or a group of friends.

Rider

When riding a pony or horse you must wear a helmet that fits you and is not damaged.

1 Dress safely for riding and know why you must wear a hard hat and suitable footwear.

2 Show how to:
   - approach a pony correctly.
   - catch a pony and put on a headcollar or halter.
   - lead a pony in hand.

3 Do all of the following.
   - Mount and dismount correctly.
   - Ride a quiet pony in an enclosed area without a leading rein.
   - Halt, walk, turn and trot safely.

4 Know how to ride along a road, cross a road and say 'thank you'.

Be safe

5 Know the basic needs of a grass-kept pony in summer and winter, such as feeding, watering and grooming.

6 Do each of the following:
   - Identify the simple points of a pony or horse.
   - Identify the simple points of a saddle and bridle.

Date

Comments

Tester

Try it this way
- You can be tested for this badge on a friend's or riding school's pony that is the right size for you.
- If you hold the Pony Club D Test Certificate or the Riding for the Disabled Proficiency Test Grade Three Award (Riding and Horse Care) you may have this badge.

Tester tips
A Brownie with a disability should take the test at a stables where she is known, riding her usual pony. She should use approved mounting facilities and any special or adapted tack if necessary. Her instructor should be present.

Road safety

1 Take a photograph or draw a picture of:
   - a safe crossing place.
   - an unsafe crossing place.
   Show you understand the differences.

2 Know the Green Cross Code and explain how to cross roads safely.

3 Do both of the following.
   - Design an outfit to help someone be easily seen when walking near roads at night or in bad weather. Describe what materials you would use and why.
   - Design a cycle helmet. Know why wearing a helmet is very important.

4 Know the order of traffic lights and what the different colours mean. Make up a game or activity for other Brownies based on traffic lights.

5 Do both of the following.
   - Look at the road signs and markings shown in *The Highway Code*. Know the difference between circular, triangular and rectangular signs. Point out one example of each and explain what they mean.
   - Explain the meaning of some signs and markings when shown a picture of them.

6 Do both of the following.
   - Know how to keep safe when going out without an adult.
   - Make a poster or game about what to do if lost or separated from your carer or friends.

Date

Comments

Tester

Need any help?
- Visit www.hedgehogs.gov.uk or www.walktoschool.org.uk for help.
- Get free road safety materials, such as *Arrive Alive – A Highway Code For Young Road Users* or plastic road signs flashcards, from www.thinkroadsafety.gov.uk.
- Ask your Leader to invite a Road Safety Officer to visit your Brownie meeting and talk about road safety: the Road Safety Department can be contacted through your local authority.

Web safe

Try it this way
You could draw, paint or use a computer programme to design your outdoor outfit. You may want to make a collage, or put on a clothes show.

Science investigator

1 Choose and carry out three of the following investigations. For each one you should keep a record of what you did and what you observed. Explain to the tester what you have found out from your results.

● Grow some salt crystals. Try making crystals using sugar. Talk with the tester about other materials that are crystals.

● Make bubble wands and bubble mix. Show how to make different bubble sizes and shapes.

● Test the different food dyes on sugar-coated sweets using chromatography.

● Make a set of coloured pastels. Explain what ingredients were used and how to make different colours and shades.

● Make natural dyes from vegetables and fruit. Dye some cotton fabric and know how to stop the dye from running when the fabric is washed.

● Make an acid indicator using red cabbage. Test the following items:
  – sugar.
  – lemonade.
  – orange juice or apple juice.
  – toothpaste.
  – yoghurt.
  – vinegar.

● Make a musical instrument and play a tune. Describe how you can make different notes and the sound louder or quieter.

● Plant some seeds in an eggshell and record what happens as they grow.

● Make a magnetic maze. Describe what happens if you use objects made from:
  – wood.
  – iron.
  – paper.
  – aluminium.
  – two materials of your choice.

● Make a balloon rocket and explain how it works.

● Using a small magnet, make your own compass. Use it to direct someone North, South, East or West.

● Build a waterproof shelter. Record what types of materials worked best to stop you getting wet.

2 Do one of the following and talk with the tester about it.

- Visit a museum, science centre, zoo, botanic garden, aquarium, science festival or other place that has a science exhibition.

- Find out about the discoveries of two scientists and how their work affects our lives.

Date
Comments

Tester

Try it this way
- The investigation records can be made using a computer programme.
- If you complete different options for both clauses you can have another Science investigator badge.

Tester tips
- If possible, complete one investigation at the test.
- One investigation for each badge may be completed at school.

Safety
Ask an adult you know for help with these activities.

Be safe

Seasons

Either

Choose and do one clause from each season.

Or

Do all the clauses from one season.

Spring

- With an adult you know, make a nest box or bird feeder. With permission, hang it in a suitable place. **Be safe**
- Tell your Six about a folk custom or religious festival that takes place during the spring. Either act it out with your Six or make some costumes for it.
- Keep a record for at least two weeks of when and where you see the following:
  - spring flowers.
  - leaves appearing on trees.
  - baby animals.
- Make a gauge to measure rainfall. Use it for at least two weeks and keep a daily record. Discuss the changes.

Summer

- Make a bird-bath and fill it each day with water. Keep a record for two weeks of the birds that use it. Make a note of any other creatures that visit it.
- Find out about sports and activities that take place in your local area during the summer. If possible, join in with one.
- Plan your ideal holiday. Make a scrapbook with pictures and information about your dream destination that you can share with your Six.
- Watch butterflies, bees and other insects on a flowering plant or bush. Know what they are doing and why. Taste three different types of honey and decide which is your favourite.

Autumn

- Know which fruits and vegetables are available in the autumn. Make something to eat using one of them, like blackberry pie or toffee apples, to share with your Six.
- Make a scrapbook or poster about animals that hibernate in this country and around the world. You can use photos and drawings as well as information.
- With an adult you know, spend time looking at the stars and point out at least two constellations.

Be safe

- Do one of the following.
  - Use fallen natural objects, like conkers, acorns or leaves, to make a collage or decoration.
  - Make a picture from bark or stone rubbing.

Winter

- Make a bird pudding and leave it out somewhere safe for birds to eat. Keep a record for at least two weeks of all the birds that eat the food.
- Know why it is important to be seen clearly when outdoors in the dark. Make reflective strips and attach them to your coat and bag.
- Tell your Six about winter festivals from two different faiths or cultures. Either help celebrate one of them, or do an activity linked with it.
- Grow a bulb, such as a hyacinth, in a clear container or water so you can see its roots grow.

Date

Comments

Tester

Try it this way

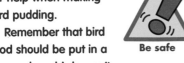

Be safe

- Ask an adult you know for help when making bird pudding.
- Remember that bird food should be put in a place where birds won't be disturbed as they eat.
- If you complete a different option from each of the four seasons, or another complete season, you can have a further Seasons badge.

Speaker

1 Prepare and present a short speech lasting about two minutes on one of the following.
- One of your hobbies.
- An event you have recently been to.
- Something you have done as a Brownie.
- A place you have visited.
- Your pet.

2 Take an active part in a group discussion, such as a Pow-wow. Explain why it is important to listen and respond to what others say.

3 Choose and read aloud a poem or short passage.

4 Do both of the following.
- Ask permission to do something.
- Thank someone for a gift or for helping you.

5 Listen to a message then repeat it to someone else without mistakes.

Date
Comments

Tester

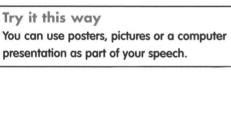

Try it this way
You can use posters, pictures or a computer presentation as part of your speech.

Sports

1 In your chosen sport, set yourself a target to improve your performance over a four-week period. This could include gaining an award or improving your speed, strength or skills. Make up a plan to help you reach your goal.

2 Keep a record of how you have:
  ● taken an active part in your chosen sport over four weeks.
  ● shown an improvement in your performance by following your plan.

3 Know the rules of your chosen sport. Discuss with the tester the importance of fair play.

4 Know how to be safe playing your sport. Show the tester:
  ● what you wear.
  ● some of the exercises you do to warm up and cool down.

5 Make a scrapbook about famous sportswomen and sportsmen who take part in your chosen sport.

Date
Comments

Tester

Try it this way
● If you choose another sport, you can work for this badge again.
● Your chosen sport can be a team, individual, combat or racquet sport.

Tester tips
The tester must be a sports instructor or teacher with knowledge of the Brownie's chosen sport.

Need any help?
Search for the website of the governing body of your chosen sport for local clubs, training courses and official rules.

Web safe

Stargazer

1 With an adult you know, go outside when it is dark and do the following.
   ● Look at the stars.
   Be safe
   ● Point out the Plough and use it to find the North Star.
   ● Point out two other constellations.
   ● Look at the stars through a telescope or binoculars. Know what are good conditions for stargazing.

2 Tell other Brownies the stories behind the two constellations you pointed out in clause 1.

3 Visit a planetarium, observatory, museum or website with an astronomy section. Tell the tester four things you found out.

4 Make a mobile or draw a picture to show the phases of our Moon.

5 Name the planets in our solar system. Find out some facts about four of them and use this to make a game or puzzle for other Brownies.

6 Explain why sailors in ancient times needed to know about the stars.

> **Date**
> **Comments**
>
> **Tester**

Try it this way
For clause 4, any art or craft method is acceptable provided the Moon's phases are shown, and the Brownie understands them.

Tester tips
● Where appropriate, the Southern Cross should be substituted for the North Star.
● A note from a parent or guardian is acceptable where appropriate.
● Brownies can make star charts of the constellations for clause 1.

Need any help?
● Planetariums and observatories sometimes run sessions for Brownies and other youth groups. Contact your local library for more information.
● For a tour of the solar system, visit http://solarsystem.jpl.nasa.gov.

Web safe

Swimmer

1 Do all of the following.
- Safely enter shallow water without using steps.
- By bending your knees, submerge yourself in shallow water ten times, breathing out each time.
- On your front, push and glide from the side or bottom of the pool to a standing position.
- Swim ten metres front crawl.
- Swim ten metres back crawl.
- Swim ten metres breaststroke.
- On either your front or your back, float for 20 seconds.
- Swim 20 metres without stopping using any strokes.

2 Do all of the following.
- Know why you should not run on the poolside.
- Know what you should do before getting into the pool.
- Be able to tell which is the shallow end and which is the deep end of a pool.
- Know what to do if you feel unwell in or near the pool, and if another swimmer is having difficulties.

Date
Comments

Tester

Tester tips
- The tester should be a qualified swimming instructor, swimming teacher or a suitably experienced adult.
- Clauses may be adapted to suit each Brownie's needs, and should remain challenging.

Try it this way
If you hold a swimming award, ask your instructor to check this syllabus to decide whether you have completed everything needed for this badge.

Swimmer advanced

You don't have to have the Swimmer badge before working for this badge.

1 Do all of the following.
- Jump into deep water and tread water for 30 seconds.
- Swim 25 metres front crawl.
- Swim 25 metres back crawl.
- Swim 25 metres breaststroke.
- Scull head first, using your hands, for ten metres.
- In water that is shoulder deep, swim through an underwater hoop.
- Demonstrate a mushroom float for ten seconds.
- Pick up an object from the pool floor.
- Swim ten metres front crawl leg kick using a float.
- Confidently swim 50 metres using any strokes without stopping.

2 Do both of the following.
- Discuss with the tester the importance of hygiene and safety rules at your regular swimming pool.
- Know where it is safe to dive into a pool and what precautions you should take before diving.

Date
Comments

Tester

Tester tips
- The tester should be a qualified swimming instructor, swimming teacher or a suitably experienced adult.
- When picking up an object from the pool floor, the water must be a minimum of 75cm deep.
- When swimming using any strokes, swimmers should only use the major competitive strokes and demonstrate a good style.
- Clauses may be adapted to suit each Brownie's needs, and should remain challenging.

Try it this way
If you hold a swimming award, ask your instructor to check this syllabus to decide whether you have completed everything needed for this badge.

Toymaker

Choose and make three items from the list below. Each item should be well made, safe and ready for use when you show it to the tester.

- A puppet, such as a glove puppet, two finger puppets, a shadow puppet, jointed puppet or something similar. Put on a short show starring your puppet.
- Accessories for a doll or teddy, like a car, house or clothes.
- A board game or jigsaw to share with your Six.

- A teddy bear or stuffed toy.
- A dressing-up costume for yourself or a friend.
- A toy that might help a younger child practise doing up buttons, using zips, tying bows and other skills.
- A toy made from materials that would have been thrown away.
- Another toy of your choice.

Try it this way
If you complete three more clauses you can have another Toymaker badge.

Date
Comments

Tester

Water safety

1 Know why the following can be dangerous.
- Outside water, such as lakes, rivers, canals and ponds.
- Shallow water.
- Cold water.
- Standing on iced-over rivers, ponds, lakes and canals.

2 Know the safety signs and flags you might see at a beach or other area of open water.

Need any help?
Visit www.lifesavers.org.uk.

Web safe

Tester tips
The tester can be any responsible person with relevant, up-to-date knowledge and experience.

Try it this way
If you hold the Rookie Lifesaver Two Star Award for Water Safety from Lifesavers (Royal Life Saving Society UK), you may have this badge.

3 Do all of the following.
- Know where it is safe to swim.
- Explain why these places are safe.
- Know why you should never swim alone.
- Explain the role of a lifeguard.

4 Name some causes of water pollution.

5 Know the Water Safety Code.

Date
Comments
Tester

Watersports

You must wear appropriate safety equipment that is in good condition when taking part in watersports.

1 Do both of the following.
   ● In a pool with lifeguard cover:
     – swim 50 metres.
     – stay afloat for five minutes.
   ● Show how to put on a personal buoyancy aid.
2 Do both of the following.
   ● Know why you should shower or wash after taking part in watersports.
   ● Know how to stop getting cold or injured when taking part in watersports.

3 Take part in at least four sessions of one of the following watersports, or a similar water activity.
   ● Canoeing.
   ● Rafting.
   ● Rowing.
   ● Sailing.
   ● Water skiing.
   ● Windsurfing.

4 For your chosen watersport:
   ● show the tester what you would wear.
   ● know the safety rules.

Date

Comments

Tester

Try it this way
If you have enjoyed taking part in a watersport, find out about the awards you could try.

Need any help?
● **British Canoe Union 18 Market Place, Bingham, Nottingham, NG13 8AP 0845 370 9500** www.bcu.org.uk
● **Amateur Rowing Association 6 Lower Mall, London, W6 9DJ 020 8237 6700** www.ara-rowing.org
● **Royal Yachting Association RYA House, Ensign Way, Hamble, Southampton, Hampshire, SO31 4YA 0845 345 0400** www.rya.org.uk

Tester tips
● Instructors must hold the appropriate qualifications required by Girlguiding UK as well as the governing body for the sport concerned.
● All appropriate Girlguiding UK rules and guidelines should be followed during the test.

Web safe

Wildlife explorer

1 Spend at least 15 minutes each day for a week watching the birds, animals and insects near where you live. Go with an adult you know to a local park, or watch what is happening in your garden or school grounds. Record what you see in a nature notebook.

Be safe

2 Identify three of each of the following.
   - Common wild birds.
   - Common butterflies.
   - Wild mammals.

3 Make a feeding station. This could be for hedgehogs, insects, birds, frogs or other creatures that aren't pets. With permission, put it up in a suitable place.

4 Choose and do one of the following.
   - Organise an RSPB Big Garden Birdwatch in your garden, local park or school grounds. Invite other Brownies, your friends or family to join in. Make a record of the birds that visit during one hour.
   - Watch for and note when migrating birds arrive for the summer or winter.
   - With an adult you know, find a pond or stream and study what lives there. Look for insects, fish, amphibians and plants. Make a record of any signs of pollution.

Be safe

   - Visit a nature reserve or country park. Draw pictures or take photographs of at least four different types of tree. Make leaf and bark rubbings. Label them with the names of the trees.

> **Date**
> **Comments**
>
>
> **Tester**

Need any help?

More information on the Big Garden Birdwatch is available from the RSPB The Lodge, Sandy, Bedfordshire, SG19 2DL 01767 680551 www.rspb.org.uk/birdwatch.

Web safe

Try it this way

- Remember that a feeding station should be put in a place where the creatures using it can eat without being disturbed.
- Don't forget to use the Country Code and Water Safety Code when outdoors.

World cultures

Choose and do five of the following.

- Make a scrapbook about your own culture. Include details that might be of interest to someone from a different country, such as:
  - your national anthem.
  - the meaning of one of your names.
  - information about your faith or religion.
  - a picture of your national flag.
  - a picture of someone in your national dress.
  - your family's or town's coat of arms.
  - your national emblem.
  - a recipe for a national dish.
  - information about a national or patron saint.
- Keep a record of the food that you eat during one week, such as:
  - the country or part of the world where you would expect to eat that food.
  - details from the packaging about where the ingredients come from.

  Point out these different places on a map of the world.

- From magazines, newspapers and websites, collect pictures that show girls and women around the world at work, school and relaxing. Include pictures from your own country.

  Web safe

- Make a decoration or craft from another country, for example Mexican God's eye, Danish heart, Swedish dove or Rangoli patterns.
- Listen to or read a story from another country. Act it out with your Six for other Brownies to watch.
- Decorate an egg in the style of an Eastern European Easter egg.
- Make some food from a culture other than your own that is eaten at a festival time, such as Saint Nicholas' biscuits eaten in Scandinavia at Christmas or Jewish New Year honey cake.
- With other Brownies, plan and take part in a Japanese doll festival, or a Chinese New Year celebration.

- Choose and do one of the following.
  - Make a mask of an animal from another part of the world.
  - Make a mask to represent a custom or tradition from a culture other than your own.
- Find out about jewellery worn around the world. Make earrings or a necklace from natural materials, or use modelling clay to simulate bone or teeth.
- Make a scrapbook about different clothes and costumes worn around the world. This could include pictures, costume dolls or clothes.

- Choose and do one of the following.
  - Play a singing game from another country.
  - Make a musical instrument from another country.
- Make a model of a house from another country. Find out what it would be built from.

Date
Comments

Tester

Try it this way

If you complete five more clauses you can have another World cultures badge.

World guiding

Choose and do five of the following.

- Learn a Brownie song from another country. Sing it with your Six.
- Make a friendship circle of paper dolls. Colour each one with a different Brownie uniform from around the world.
- Take part in an event or activity with Brownies from another unit.
- Say hello to a Brownie you don't know. Give her something you have made.
- Find out what WAGGGS stands for. Draw the World Badge and explain what each part means.
- Explain what it means to you to know there are Brownies in so many different countries.
- Draw or glue a picture of one of the four World Centres on to card. Make it in to a jigsaw puzzle for another Brownie to complete.
- Know something about each of the four World Centres.

- Send a postcard, tape, letter or email to a Brownie in another country. You can do this on your own or with other Brownies.
- Cook and taste something that a Brownie in another Commonwealth country might regularly eat.
- Design a World Thinking Day card. Send it to someone you know in guiding.
- With other Brownies, plan and take part in a World Thinking Day celebration.
- Talk with someone who has been abroad with Girlguiding UK. Tell the tester what you found out.
- Choose a country where there are Brownies. Make a poster and use it to tell your Six about the country and the Brownies who live there.

Date
Comments

Tester

Need any help?
- **Visit WAGGGS' website www.wagggs.org** for details about the World Centres.
- **Details of World Thinking Day, as well as a jump station with links to Girl Guide and Girl Scout organisations in other countries, can be found at Girlguiding UK's website www.girlguiding.org.uk.**

Web safe

Try it this way
If you complete five more clauses you can have another World guiding badge.

World issues

Choose and do five of the following.

- Plant a tree in your local area.
  - Know why trees are important to the air we breathe.
  - Show on a map of the world where trees are in danger.
  - Describe what a sustainable forest is.
- Take some cans, bottles, newspapers or clothes to be recycled. Find out how they will be recycled and know why this is good for the world's environment.
- For a week keep a record of how much water you use each day and what you use the water for. Make a poster showing how a water shortage may affect you. With your Six, taste different types of clean safe water, like tap water, filtered water and bottled water. Agree which one is your favourite.
- Draw the flag or symbol of an organisation that helps people around the world. Make a leaflet about the work it does and how others can support it.

- Find out about the Olympic Games, Winter Olympics, Special Olympics or Paralympics. Know how the Games started and their role in the world.
- Spot three differences and three similarities between you and a Brownie friend. Discuss with the tester if you think the differences are important. Find out three things you have in common with Brownies in other countries.
- Make a meal using an ingredient grown in another country, like bananas, pineapple, coffee or chocolate.
- Find out about Fair Trade. Do a survey of Fair Trade products that you can buy locally. Make a drink or snack using one of the products.
- Talk with the tester about how a war may start. Discuss how war affects people's lives.
- Name three countries with languages different from yours and each other's. Show how you would communicate with a person from each country.

- Show how to wash your hands and clean your teeth properly. Know why it is important to do these things regularly and what you would do in a country where it is difficult to get clean water.
- Play a game from another country. Make up a game of your own and explain the rules to your Six.
- Make a poster about children's rights. Play a game with other Brownies then talk with them about why rules and fair play are important.

- Find out about an international aid organisation like UNICEF, Oxfam or the Red Crescent. Tell the tester:
  - when it was started.
  - why it began.
  - what it is trying to do for people around the world.

Date
Comments

Tester

Tester tips
A note from a parent or guardian is acceptable where appropriate.

Try it this way
If you complete five more clauses you can have another World issues badge.

Need any help?
- For information about the Olympics visit www.specialolympics.org, www.paralympic.org and www.olympic.org.
- For more on the London Olympics, visit www.london2012.org.
- For details on Fair Trade visit www.fairtrade.org.uk.
- Ask your Leader about some of the activities that appear in Girlguiding UK's publication *Right Now*.

Web safe

World traveller

Choose and do five of the following.

- Choose a country with a language other than your own. Learn to say:
  - numbers one to ten.
  - hello.
  - thank you.
  - goodbye.
- Know what you should remember to do when walking or cycling in a different country.
- Show you can tell that a car is from a different country.
- Show how you might greet people from three countries in their traditional way, such as rubbing noses (Canadian Inuits), the wai (Thailand) or peace sign (Native Americans).
- Know why people have passports. Make a pretend one for yourself containing a photo or drawing of yourself, your name, date of birth and address. Draw in entry stamps from different countries.
- Help to plan and take a trip on a bus, train, boat or plane. Draw a picture or make a scrapbook showing what you enjoyed. Discuss with the tester the plans you would make to travel to another country.

- With an adult you know, cook something on a camp fire or barbecue, like marshmallows, sausages or bananas. Explain to the tester the type of food you would carry and cook when travelling.

Be safe

- Pack a small bag with the things you need to stay away from home for one night. Don't forget a game to play, something to read or your cuddly toy.
- On a day trip or holiday take some photographs. Display and label them, or arrange them in an album.
- Collect some souvenirs from abroad. Use them to play Kim's Game with your Six.
- Make a postcard to send to a friend. On a piece of card, draw or stick a picture of a place. On the back tell your friend about what the place is like and what you did there.
- Show the tester what type of clothes you might wear if you lived in:
  - a very cold country.
  - a very hot country.
  - a very wet country.
  - a very dry country.

Date
Comments

Tester

Writer

1 Write one of the following.
- A poem that is not longer than 20 lines.
- A story of your own.
- A song that you could teach your Six then all sing to other Brownies.

2 Choose and do two of the following.
- Write an article for a magazine about something exciting you have done in Brownies.
- Write a scene for your favourite television or radio programme.
- Write a description around 500 words long about your favourite person, television celebrity, actor, popstar or Brownie friend.
- Keep a diary for four weeks. Record your thoughts and feelings, and what you did.

- Put together a glossary (words and their meanings) of at least ten words to do with one of your hobbies, such as Brownies, cooking, swimming, singing or computers.
- Write a letter inviting someone to a Promise Celebration at Brownies explaining what the celebration is about.

Date
Comments

Tester

Try it this way
- The diary can be written as an Internet blog.
- If you complete different options for both clauses you can have another Writer badge.

Web safe

Tester tips
- The tester should have time before the test to read your writing.
- Include a letter from a parent, guardian or teacher confirming that the pieces are your own, unaided work.
- One item for each badge may be written at school.
- Clauses may be adapted to suit each Brownie, and should remain challenging.
- Brownies may write using a computer.

FROM BROWNIE WEAR TO GREAT GIFTS WE ARE THE PLACE TO SHOP

ALL OUR CLOTHES ARE MACHINE WASHABLE

GILET
65% polyester, 35% cotton.
To fit chest
3161 24"/61cm **3162** 26"/66cm
3163 28"/71cm **3164** 30"/76cm
3165 32"/81cm **3166** 34"/86cm
3167 36"/91cm

TROUSERS
100% polyester. To fit waist
3168 20"/51cm **3169** 22"/56cm
3170 24"/61cm **3171** 26"/66cm
3172 28"/71cm **3173** 30"/76cm
3174 32"/81cm **3199** 34"/86cm

LONG-SLEEVED T-SHIRT
100% polyester. To fit chest
3147 24"/61cm **3148** 26"/66cm
3149 28"/71cm **3150** 30"/76cm
3151 32"/81cm **3152** 34"/86cm
3153 36"/91cm

CYCLING SHORTS
92% cotton, 8% elastane.
To fit waist
3189 20"/51cm **3190** 22"/56cm
3191 24"/61cm **3192** 26"/66cm
3193 28"/71cm **3194** 30"/76cm
3197 32"/81cm

SHORT-SLEEVED T-SHIRT
100% cotton. To fit chest
3140 24"/61cm **3141** 26"/66cm
3142 28"/71cm **3143** 30"/76cm
3144 32"/81cm **3145** 34"/86cm
3146 36"/91cm

SKORT
100% polyester. To fit waist
3175 20"/51cm **3176** 22"/56cm
3177 24"/61cm **3178** 26"/66cm
3179 28"/71cm **3180** 30"/76cm
3181 32"/81cm

HOODED ZIP JACKET
65% polyester, 35% cotton.
To fit chest
3154 24"/61cm **3155** 26"/66cm
3156 28"/71cm **3157** 30"/76cm
3158 32"/81cm **3159** 34"/86cm
3160 36"/91cm

LEGGINGS
92% cotton, 8% elastane.
To fit waist
3182 20"/51cm **3183** 22"/56cm
3184 24"/61cm **3185** 26"/66cm
3186 28"/71cm **3187** 30"/76cm
3188 32"/81cm

BROWNIE DUVET SET
50% cotton, 50% polyester
2414

CERAMIC MUG
2388

BROWNIE TEDDY
Height: 21cm 2599

BROWNIE SLING BAG
Size: 24cm x 29cm 2451

BAG CHARM
7061